ALL-COLOUR WOK RECIPES

Peter Nikolay

LONDON • NEW YORK • TORONTO • SYDNEY

foulsham

Contents

Foreword

No other cooking utensil is quite as versatile as the Wok for the preparation of both Asiatic and European food. It offers speed in a variety of cooking methods and helps food to retain its nutritional value, colour and texture.

Many recipes in this book are based on modern European wok cooking together with Asian, although strong-tasting ingredients have, to some extent, been deliberately omitted. Additionally, I have included some Vietnamese and Thai dishes which I learned how to cook during my stay in Paris over a number of years. Most are based on the use of fresh ingredients seasoned delicately with herbs and spices, similar to the high quality Eastern food one finds not only in Paris, but all the major European cities.

As with all wok dishes, ingredients that are fresh and of top quality are a must because the relatively short cooking time quickly reveals the taste of stale or inferior food. It is therefore advisable to select seasonal fresh or frozen food of high quality and use substitutes where indicated if the first choice is unavailable.

I hope that cooking with a wok will provide you with as much pleasure as it has given me, and I wish you much success with my recipes

Peter Nikolay

3

The Wok

The History of the Wok

The wok is a Chinese invention with a long tradition. It is difficult to establish exactly when the wok first appeared on the scene, but possibly it began life in farm kitchens where it was used to prepare simple meals quickly.

Due to its half-spherical shape, it required only a small source of heat and, with the addition of a firm ring, it acquired an indispensable stand. In this way it became possible for ordinary people to cook without difficulty, even in the fields. In a figurative sense it could be likened to a small, portable, low-heat oven.

From the fields and the farm kitchens the wok quickly found its way into the large palace kitchens where it became a classic cooking utensil valued by everyone.

The Asian art of cooking developed progressively throughout the centuries before maturing to its present classicism. It is therefore not surprising that Asian cooking, and especially cooking with the wok, has found favour in the West.

The Right Equipment

The secret of all good cooking is to use best quality ingredients and proper cooking equipment. This ensures maximum success.

The name wok comes from Cantonese and means simply cooking vessel. It is a frying pan with a spherical base and high sides and the original wok was used exclusively on an open fire, standing on top of a special support ring. It had an outer rounded base which prevented it from shifting its position and tipping over.

Due to its spherical shape, heat from the wok spreads from the base upwards along the high sides. If, during cooking, the ingredients are continually stirred, they will all

receive even distribution of heat. Meat and fish will thus retain their juices and vegetables their colour, taste and vitamins. To adapt the wok to modern European kitchens, many now have a flatter base which suits a gas or electric hob.

If you are generally cooking for four people, choose a wok with a top measurement of about 35 cm/14 in. If the wok is too small, food could spill over the sides while being stir-fried. Bigger tends to be better.

Types of Wok
The material from which the wok is made is most important and it is essential that it should be a good conductor of heat while, at the same time, sturdy enough to conserve it. Non-stick, stainless steel and cast iron all give reliable service but make sure whichever wok chosen has wooden or firm plastic handles which stay cool to the touch. It also needs a lid for steaming and to hold in the heat.

Cast Iron Woks

Cast iron woks have the distinct advantage of retaining heat for a long time, ensuring that cooked food stays warm. Because cast iron is heavier than most other metals, the wok will stay in place during vigorous stirring of ingredients. These woks do require a little more care and attention when cleaning compared with those made of other materials. After cooking, rinse with warm water and wipe dry. Afterwards grease with a little oil before storing.

Stainless Steel Woks

Some stainless steel woks look impressive in a modern kitchen, elegant and gleaming, and they perform well.

Electric Woks

For cooking in a congenial atmosphere the electric wok can be a great boon. Every guest can cook food according to personal taste or one can conjure up an original dish for everyone.

Non-Stick Woks

Non-stick coated woks have the advantage of being easy to clean. however, metal spatulas should not be used for stirring.

Wok for Singles

For small households and singles, a somewhat smaller wok has recently become available with a diameter of just 28 cm/11 in. It is quite handy and is adequate for two servings.

Caring for your Wok

As important as buying a good wok is its care afterwards.

Before using your new wok, wash it well using hot water and detergent. Wipe round with a sponge, rinse again and wipe dry with a soft tea towel. Brush the inside with groundnut or sunflower oil. Heat until hot, cool down slightly and wipe out with kitchen paper.

Rinse with hot water before using but avoid detergent which will remove the film of oil on the inside. Pat dry with paper towels. Alternatively, follow the maker's directions regarding care.

Do not season non-stick woks.

Wok Accessories

For cooking with a wok, various accessories are available.

There is a wire inset that can be fitted on top of the wok, and serves as a drainer and as a means of keeping cooked food warm.

Indispensable for stir-frying in the wok is a spatula, which should ideally be made from wood to prevent scratching the inside, especially if the wok is non-stick.

A wooden chopstick can also be used instead of a spatula. The sieve or perforated spoon is used to remove already cooked ingredients from the cooking stock or sauce, as this enables the liquid to drip away easily through the small holes.

Besides frying, braising and deep-frying, the wok can also be used for steaming. For this you will need a bamboo steaming basket which can be found in assorted sizes from kitchen shops or Asian shops. The bamboo weave is made in such a way that steam can penetrate well inside the basket. The steaming basket is placed inside the wok with a little water, which must be shallow enough not to touch the basket. The lid is then placed on the wok and the ingredients steamed, in similar fashion to a pressure cooker or traditional steamer.

If you want to serve food straight from the wok, then a 'rechaud' is an essential piece of equipment. It is obtainable from specialist shops and has a spirit burner or a cartridge fuel burner. It is important to make sure that the burner is compatible with your size of wok and has a good stand.

Rice has always been at the centre of every meal in Asian cooking and serves as the best accompaniment to most of the main meals in this book. On page 17 you will find a number of basic recipes for the preparation of rice. For enthusiasts of non-sticky rice, a special piece of equipment has recently become available in the shops – an electric rice cooker. It helps the cook to produce perfect rice every time and to keep it warm while waiting to be served. For those not quite so keen on kitchen gadgets, you can achieve perfect results with a simple saucepan!

Cooking Methods

Before You Cook

Preparation of Ingredients
Cut up all the ingredients –
for instance the meat and
vegetables – into cubes, slices
or strips as stated in the
recipe, before you begin to
cook. The smaller the pieces,
the shorter the cooking times
will be. Place the prepared
cooking ingredients
separately into small dishes
alongside the wok so that
everything is readily access-
ible when needed.

Preparing the Wok
First of all, heat up 15 ml/
1 tbsp of oil in the wok, swirl
it around then pour it out
again
(the best place is into a heat-
resistant container standing
alongside the wok). Repeat
this procedure once more.
This pre-preparation is
extremely important as it pre-
vents ingredients sticking to
the wok during cooking.

Organisation
When adding ingredients to
the wok, start with those
which will take longest to
cook, adding the more tender
ingredients afterwards. This
technique helps to ensure
that the ingredients stay firm,
do not overcook and are all
ready at the same time.

Stir-Frying

This is the favourite and quic-
kest method of cooking in a
wok as the ingredients retain
their flavour and colour and
are cooked until tender but
still crisp. Due to the high
temperature, the ingredients
are sealed immediately when
added so that juices are loc-
ked in. The meat, for instance,
thus stays moist while the
outside remains crisp. When
using this method it is particularly important that all
ingredients are cut into pieces
of about the same size and
that the oil in the wok is very
hot. First, put the ingredients
with the longest cooking time
in the wok (this is usually the
meat) and fry, stirring continually. Only in this way can
the heat reach all surfaces of
the small pieces ensuring that
they will be evenly cooked.
The shape of the wok is par-
ticuarly suitable for this
technique and frying
rarely lasts longer than a few
minutes. Remove the fried
ingredients from the wok and
keep them warm. Then add
the other ingredients (usually
the vegetables) and fry, stirring in the same way. Add the
sauce if called for. Finally, put
everything back into the wok,
reheat and stir carefully once
more, making sure that
everything is well mixed.
Chicken Breast with Almonds,
Lychees and Mango (see page
37), for example, is prepared
using this method. Some-
times each ingredient will be
fried separately or only a few
ingredients fried together.
They are then removed from
the wok and kept warm. Afterwards the sauce is made and
the ingredients are added and
reheated.

Simmering

In a wok, food can be sim-
mered just the same as it can
in a saucepan. This cooking
method is usually used in the
preparation of soups.
First, fry the ingredients
needed for the soup in a little
oil until brown, having pre-
viously cut them up small,
then pour on the liquid sug-
gested in the recipe. Afterwards simmer everything
together as directed but take
care the ingredients do not
overcook and remain firm to
the bite. The meat, however,
should be thoroughly cooked.
It is always important to keep
the liquid just under boiling
point and not allow it to bub-
ble up and boil. An example
of cooking by this method is
Fennel Soup with Pine Kernels
(see page 18).

Chinese Braising

This method of cooking is similar to the more common method of braising in a saucepan — it is just much quicker in a wok.

Fry the ingredients quickly so that the juices are sealed in. Afterwards pour on the liquid or sauce given in the recipe and braise for the recommended time. Do not close the wok with a lid, as the sauce will be reduced by the heat and the flavour strengthened. It is important to stir from time to time during cooking so that the sauce does not stick to the wok. An example of this method is found in Pork with Mild Pepperoni (see page 30).

Deep-Frying

For this method, the ingredients, usually pastry pockets or foods covered in pastry or batter, are fried in deep oil. The cooking time is determined by the size of the ingredients. It is important that the oil is really hot so that the batter or pastry is rapidly sealed and does not absorb excess oil. When the ingredients have become golden-brown, remove them with a slotted spoon and leave to drain well on a piece of kitchen towel resting in a bowl or on a plate. An example of this method is Spring Rolls with Coconut and Chicken (see page 40).

Steaming

This method is particularly recommended for cooking vegetables, meat and fish. For this you will need a large wok with a lid and the steaming basket that we have already described. It should be smaller in diameter than the wok.

First of all the wok is filled with a little water and then brought to the boil. Place the ingredients on a flat plate a little smaller than the basket and then place this inside the basket in the wok. Then put on the lid and steam the ingredients until soft. During cooking, remove the lid as little as possible and always ensure that there is sufficient water in the wok for it not to boil dry.

7

Special Ingredients

Fruit, Vegetables and Fresh Mushrooms

Aubergines

There are many different types of aubergines. In Britain, it is the large purple one that is best known and these can be diced and used in wok recipes.

In Asian shops, the smaller green type can also be found (1), known as large and small makeur, as well as the larger green aubergines. Large makeur (2) are round to oval and are about the size of an apricot. Around the area of the stalk they are green and towards the fruit the colour changes to white. Large makeur come from Asia, but these days they are also grown in Europe. Small makeur (3) are about the size of a cherry and the fruit is green. This type of aubergine is cultivated in Asia. As aubergines have almost no taste of their own, dishes prepared with them always need plenty of seasoning. For cooking in a wok, the small fruit should be used whenever possible. They should be halved or quartered but not peeled.

Bamboo Shoots

Bamboo shoots (4) are used in a variety of ways in Asian cooking. Used in China are young sprouts not yet woody, and green shoots. The short round and pointed shoots are available fresh, covered in pale leaves which should be removed before preparation begins. Bamboo shoots possess their own slightly bitter taste and are usually diced or cut into strips when cooked. In Britain they are rarely obtainable fresh, but are available halved or cut into strips in cans.

8

Blue Potatoes
Also called Chinese potatoes, (5) these come mostly from Asia, but recently have begun to be grown in Europe. They are only available from specialist Asian food stores. They are prepared in the same way as ordinary potatoes.

Chilli Peppers
Chilli peppers (6) are available in different sizes as well as various colours and whether they are green, yellow or red depends on their state of ripeness. In taste they can be mild or very hot; the smaller pods are hottest. For the European palate the larger pods are recommended. Before use they should be cut in two and the small seeds and the fibrous interiors removed as they are the spiciest. After this the pods should be cut up finely as described in the relevant recipe. Chilli peppers are also available dried. The dried peppers should be cooked whole as they give the dish a special piquancy. However, be very careful how many chillis you use, and remember the longer the pods are cooked, the hotter will be the taste of the dish. Try one pod first of all and only add more after tasting. Wash your hands thoroughly after preparing these spicy peppers.

Baby Sweetcorn
These (7) look the same as any other corn on the cob, but they are only about 8 cm/ 3 in long and have a somewhat milder taste than their larger brother. They are obtainable fresh in well-stocked supermarkets, frozen or in cans. Make sure you do not buy canned pickled sweetcorn as this does not have the same flavour. Keep fresh sweetcorn in the refrigerator.

Spring Onions
Available all the year round, the familiar spring onions (8) are much used in Chinese cooking instead of ordinary onions. Both white and green parts are used in Chinese recipes. Spring onions need to be used fairly quickly as they tend to go limp. Kept in the refrigerator, they will remain fresh for about two days.

9

Lychees

The fruit of a tree from South China, lychees (1) grow in panicles that can be made up of as many as 20 fruit. They can be obtained fresh practically all the year round in supermarkets or Asian shops. Before use, the firm peel should be removed. The fruit should then be halved and the dark kernel removed. Lychees can be eaten raw or cooked lightly. If unavailable fresh, use canned lychees in natural juice rather than syrup. Because they are fairly sweet and fragrant, lychees should be used only for sweet and sour dishes.

Pak Soi

Also called pak choi (2) or Japanese cabbage, this has very tender, delicate leaves, so it should never be cooked longer than necessary otherwise its fine taste is lost. For cooking, either whole leaves can be used, or the cabbage can be cut into 1 cm/½ in strips. Pak soi is suitable for deep freezing. First blanch the leaves quickly in boiling water, leave to drain, pack in foil or film and freeze. If unavailable, chicory or Chinese leaves make a reasonable substitute.

Marsh Samphire

Marsh samphire (3) or sea fennel is a type of green seaweed which is naturally salty. The French call it cornichon de mer and it is pickled in vinegar. In the UK it is rare but may be found in select fishmongers or good stores with exotic food departments.

Black Walnuts

These are actually unripe walnuts (4) left to ripen in the

shell until black. You can buy them in jars preserved in brine, when the whole nuts become deliciously soft and edible.

Shiitake Mushrooms

These mushrooms (5) are very delicately flavoured. They are available both fresh and dried. Their flesh is firm and juicy. Fresh mushrooms need only to be wiped with a damp cloth before preparation and the stalk cut back a little. When using dried shiitake mushrooms, which have almost as much taste as the fresh ones, they must first be soaked in lukewarm water until soft but it is best to be guided by the directions on the packet. Before using, the hard stalks must be cut off as they are too tough to be eaten.

10

Soy Beansprouts

Fresh, crisp and rich in vitamins and minerals, beansprouts (6) are readily available. As they are very tender, they should only be cooked for a short time. They should not be confused with mung beansprouts which are smaller and somewhat bitter. Soy beansprouts can be obtained fresh in wholefood shops, supermarkets and Asian shops as well as canned. You can easily grow them yourself. Sprouting takes from 3 to 4 days.

Tamarillos

These long egg-shaped tropical fruits (7) grow to about 9 cm/3½ in long and have an orange to brown-red inedible coloured peel. The fruit of the flesh is yellow to red and becomes softer nearer the middle. The jelly-like flesh in the centre, along with the dark seeds, can be eaten raw or cooked. Tamarillos have a pleasant tangy-sweet taste that is vaguely reminiscent of tomatoes. They are only sold in specialist stores.

Trumpet Mushrooms

These small black forest mushrooms (8), also known as autumn trumpets, are only available fresh in late summer until the winter, although they can be bought dried from specialist food stores.

Water Chestnuts

Water chestnuts (9) are small round tubers, found growing at the root end of the water chestnut plant. They have a firm, white and crisp flesh and a characteristically sweet taste. They are available in cans. Water chestnuts can be used for dishes either whole or cut into slices. Should you have any left over, they should be kept in a glass container of water in the refrigerator, and the water changed daily.

Spices, Seasonings and Herbs

Oyster Sauce
Made from fermented fish, mussels and oysters, oyster sauce (1) is somewhat thicker than other Asiatic seasoning sauces. It is available in most well-stocked supermarkets, delicatessens or Asian shops. Use it sparingly as it has a strong flavour.

Basil
A classic herb, basil (2) cannot be left out of Asian or European cooking. Asiatic basil has a milder taste than ours. Use it sparingly.

Curry Paste
Curry paste (3) is available in a range of colourings and is used for flavouring. It is easy to make yourself (see pages 16-17).

Curry Powder
A mixture of several different spices, curry powder (4) is also used widely in European cooking. It is best to use English or Indian made curry powder, as these types have a good taste and at the same time are not bitter.

Fish Sauce
Fish sauce (5) is indispensable in Thai and Vietnamese cooking. It is made from fermented shrimps and fish and serves mostly as a substitute for salt. The best quality is recognisable by a clear, brown colour that looks a bit like sweet sherry.

Turmeric
Turmeric (6) is an orange-coloured powder with a gentle taste, similar to mild ginger. It is made from a root, peeled and then finely grated, and is used to colour and season dishes.

Ginger Root
Ginger (7) is used a great deal in Asian cooking. Young, fresh root ginger is peeled and then grated, finely chopped, or cut into thin slices and used for seasoning. Root ginger can be wrapped in a damp cloth, overwrapped with film then stored for a week or so in the refrigerator. Dried ground ginger is not really a good substitute and preserved or crystalised ginger is suitable only for sweet dishes.

Chinese Chives
Chinese chives or chive garlic (8) belongs to the same group of herbs. The leaves are similar to ordinary chives and have a mild taste of garlic. It is used like chives and fresh chives or garlic make a good substitute.

Coconut Cream
Coconut cream (9) is available in cans. Use one with a creamy consistency which is unsweetened. Blocks of creamed coconut and cans of coconut milk are not the same. It is used largely for soups and sauces as well as for flavouring dishes.

If you wish, you can also make it yourself. Take a fresh coconut, cut it in two and scrape out the white flesh with a spoon or a knife. Purée the flesh with an equal amount of boiling water in a blender and pass the purée through a sieve. Leave to stand for 20 minutes until the thin liquid milk has settled at the bottom of the container. Skim off the cream. The thin liquid milk can, if necessary, be used for thinning the cream or flavouring dishes. It is best if the coconut cream is made beforehand and then frozen in portions.

Coriander Leaves
Coriander leaves (10) are a deep green herb with a specific and unmistakable flavour, available in supermarkets and Asian shops. Coriander seeds *do not* make a satisfactory substitute.

Mango Chutney
A spicy, fruity compôte that can be used as a side dish or cooking ingredient, mango chutney (11) is available in hot or sweet types which you can use according to taste. A good quality apricot jam, hotted up with mustard, makes a reasonable substitute.

Horseradish Paste

Horseradish paste (12) is a Japanese product made of green horseradish sprouts. It tastes somewhat stronger and sharper than European freshly grated horseradish and should therefore be used with great care. Our own horseradish makes an adequate substitute.

Mushroom Sauce

Made of dried black Asian mushrooms, this sauce has a strong taste. Soy sauce can also be used as a substitute.

Plum Wine

Plum wine is a sweet aromatic wine with a fine plum flavour. It can be substituted by a full-bodied red wine.

Rice Wine

One of the oldest Chinese spirits, rice wine is produced from rice, yeast and water. In shops it sometimes goes under the name of Shaoxing wine (Shao Hsing). Rice wine can be substituted by a dry to medium sherry.

Rice Schnaps

Rice schnaps is made from the same ingredients as rice wine. Instead of rice schnaps, use any good quality schaps or grappa.

Sambal Manis

This is a seasoning paste made of dried onions, fried chillis, salt, sugar and lemon juice and has a pleasantly mild taste (13). If sambal oelek (see overleaf) is too sharp for you, then this milder variation should be exactly right.

Sambal Oelek

This is a very sharp seasoning paste made of red chillis, vinegar and salt (1). When using it for seasoning, please be careful as it is hot and strong — a pinch is plenty on the tip of a spoon. Sambal oelek is readily available from oriental food shops.

Sate Powder

Sate powder (2) is a mixture of lemon grass, chillis, star anis, salt, sugar and coriander. It is available in Asian shops. You can substitute Chinese five-spice powder.

Shrimp Paste

Shrimp paste (3) is a strong-tasting seasoning paste made from salted dried shrimps. It is used largely for curries and dips because of its distinctive flavour. Keep shrimp paste in a tightly-closed container for flavour retention. It is available in Asian shops. Unfortunately it has no substitute.

Soy Sauce

Soy sauce (4) is an indispensable seasoning in Asian cooking. It is made of fermented yellow soya beans together with wheat, barley, salt, sugar and yeast and is available in almost every food store. There is dark soy sauce that is coloured with sugar, and light-coloured sauce. In Asia, on the other hand, many other types are used. For the recipes in this book we recommend the light-coloured sauce. The dark, slightly bitter-sweet tasting variety should only be used sparingly.

Star Anis

Star anis (5) is an exotic spice, the taste of which reminds one of aniseed. It is used for many Asian recipes and is also an ingredient in many spice mixtures. It is best to use a complete piece of anis as the powder often has a very intense flavour which can be overpowering.

Lemon Leaves

These (6) are typical of Thai cooking. They come from the Kaffir lemon tree, have a distinctive flavour and are used exclusively as a seasoning during cooking. Before serving the dish, the leaves should be removed. They can usually be obtained in Asian or in specialist fruit and vegetable shops and should be well-washed before use. Lemon grass can be used instead of the leaves, or even a little lemon peel.

Lemon Grass

Lemon grass (7) is a reed-like grass that has a lemon aroma and is used for flavouring. If you cannot find lemon grass, use a little grated lemon rind instead.

14

Dried Products

Seaweed Products
Dried seaweeds such as wakame (1) are much used in Asian cooking. They have very few calories, but much fibre and help digestion. They should be soaked in water for some time so that they become soft. If they are to be cooked for a long time, then this pre-soaking is not necessary.

Chinese Egg Noodles
These look very much like our own noodles (2) and taste almost the same. They are available pressed into blocks or put together in little bundles. Of course, you can substitute ordinary egg noodles for your dishes.

Chinese Dried Mushrooms
Dried mushrooms (3) are a favourite in Asian cooking, and are available from most well-stocked supermarkets or Asian shops. All dried mushrooms should first be softened in lukewarm water and for guidance, follow the directions on the packet. If the mushrooms are to be cooked for a long time in liquid, then it will not be necessary to soak them first. Do not forget that the size of the mushrooms will be much larger after they have been soaked, so always use a container large enough to allow them to swell to at least twice their size. Once soaked, discard the stems which are too hard to eat.

Noodles
Bean noodles (4) are made from ground mung beans and

are completely neutral in taste. They will, however, absorb the flavours of other ingredients and spices. Before preparation they are either left to soften for about 5 minutes in cold water then soaked and cooked, or deep-fried raw in hot oil.

Lily Buds
Lily buds (5), just like dried mushrooms, must be soaked before use. They are only available from specialist food stores.

Rice Leaves
Rice leaves (6) are used exclusively for pastry pockets and can be either fried or steamed. Before further use the leaves must first be soaked individually in water so that they become soft. Then they are taken out and

laid side by side on a piece of kitchen towel. Rice leaves are available in various sizes from Asian shops.

Rice and Potato Flours
Rice and potato flour (8) are frequently used in Asian cooking for coating meat and thickening sauces. These products are available from supermarkets and food shops.

Black Beans
Black beans (9) are small fermented and dried soy beans. Before use they must be soaked for about 2 hours in cold water and then cooked for 40 minutes in water.

Herb Chilli Sauce

Ingredients	Metric/Imperial
Green chilli peppers, chopped	6
Spring onion, chopped	1
Ginger root, chopped	5 ml/1 tsp
Cloves garlic, chopped	2
Cucumber, chopped	50 g/2 oz
Carrot, finely chopped	25 g/1 oz
Lemon grass chopped	1 stick
Coriander, finely chopped	1 sprig
Wine vinegar	20 ml/4 tsp
Sugar	10 ml/2 tsp
Fish sauce	45 ml/3 tsp
Mineral water	

1. Stir all the finely chopped ingredients together with the vinegar, sugar and fish sauce and dilute to taste with mineral water.

Red Chilli Sauce

Ingredients	Metric/Imperial
Shallots, diced	100 g/4 oz
Red chilli peppers, halved	8
Cloves garlic, crushed	4
Fish sauce	30 ml/2 tsp
Brown sugar	15 ml/1 tsp
Juice of lemons	2
Mineral water	

1. Roast the finely chopped ingredients slowly in the wok until golden brown. Purée with the fish sauce, sugar and lemon juice in a blender. Dilute with mineral water as required.

Chilli-Spice Sauce

Ingredients	Metric/Imperial
Shallots, diced	3
Cloves garlic, diced	6
Root ginger, chopped	25 g/1 oz
Red chilli peppers, halved	8
Groundnut oil	15 ml/1 tbsp
Coriander seeds	10 ml/2 tsp
Coriander, chopped	1 sprig
Shrimp paste	10 ml/2 tsp
Wine vinegar	10 ml/2 tsp
Fish sauce	30 ml/2 tbsp
Soft brown sugar	30 ml/2 tbsp
Mineral water	

1. Roast the shallots, garlic, ginger and chilli peppers in a little oil in the wok until golden brown. Purée to a smooth paste in a blender with all the remaining ingredients except the mineral water. Dilute as required with mineral water.

Yellow Curry Paste

Ingredients	Metric/Imperial
Red chilli peppers, halved	2
Yellow chilli peppers, halved	10
Coriander seeds	10 ml/2 tsp
Caraway seeds	5 ml/1 tsp
Turmeric	10 ml/2 tsp
Cloves	5
Lemon grass, chopped	2 sticks
Cinnamon	1 stick
Shallots, finely chopped	3
Cloves garlic, chopped	10
Root ginger, chopped	15 g/½ oz
Salt	5 ml/1 tsp
Shrimp paste	10 ml/2 tsp
Mineral water	

1. Lightly roast the chilli peppers in the wok until light brown with the coriander, caraway, turmeric, cloves, lemon grass and cinnamon. Purée in a blender with the shallots, garlic, ginger, salt and shrimp paste. Dilute with mineral water until spreadable.

Green Curry Paste

Ingredients	Metric/Imperial
Green chilli peppers,	20
Grated nutmeg	5 ml/1 tsp
Cinnamon	1 stick
Lemon grass, chopped	2 sticks
Coriander seeds	5 ml/1 tsp
Caraway seeds	2.5 ml/½ tsp
Cloves garlic, chopped	10
Shallots, finely chopped	3
Coriander	1 sprig
Basil	1 sprig
Spinach leaves, chopped	50 g/2 oz
Salt	5 ml/1 tsp
Shrimp paste	10 ml/2 tsp
Mineral water	

1. Roast the chilli peppers lightly in the wok until light brown with nutmeg, cinnamon, lemon grass, coriander and caraway seeds. Purée until smooth in a blender with the garlic, shallots, fresh herbs, spinach, shrimp paste and salt. Dilute the paste with a little mineral water.

Red Curry Paste

Ingredients	Metric/Imperial
Red chilli peppers, halved	15
Coriander seeds	10 ml/2 tsp
Caraway seeds	5 ml/1 tsp
Cinnamon	1 stick
Grated nutmeg	10 ml/2 tsp
Mace (optional)	2 blades
Lemon grass, chopped	2 sticks
Lemon leaves, chopped	2
Root ginger chopped	50 g/2½ oz
Shallots, finely chopped	3
Salt	5 ml/1 tsp
Shrimp paste	10 ml/2 tsp
Mineral water	

1. Lightly roast the chilli peppers in the wok until light brown with coriander, caraway, cinnamon, nutmeg, mace if used, lemon grass and lemon leaves. Purée in a blender with the ginger, shallots, salt and shrimp paste. Dilute the mixture with a little mineral water.

Thai Scented Rice

Ingredients	Metric/Imperial
Thai scented rice	250 g/9 oz
Water	900 ml/1½ pts
A pinch of salt	

1. Wash the rice well. Bring to the boil in salted water, cover and simmer for 20 minutes over a low heat. Fluff up the grains with a fork before serving.

Serves 4

Thai Coconut Rice

Ingredients	Metric/Imperial
Thai scented rice	250 g/9 oz
Coconut milk	1 l/1¾ pts
Coconut cream	150 ml/¼ pt
Coriander, chopped	1 sprig
A pinch of salt	

1. Wash the rice well. Bring to the boil in a saucepan with the coconut milk and the cream, the coriander and a little salt. Put on the lid and let the rice swell for 20 to 25 minutes over a low heat, stirring occasionally.

Serves 4

Spiced Rice

Ingredients	Metric/Imperial
Olive oil	15 ml/1 tsp
Shallots, finely chopped	2
Carrot, finely chopped	1
Leek, finely chopped	1
Medium grain rice	250 g/9 oz
Poultry stock	900 ml/1½ pts
Dry white wine	30 ml/2 tbsp
Salt	
A pinch of nutmeg	
Chopped fresh parsley	

1. Heat the oil and fry the vegetables until transparent. Add the rice and fry for about 5 minutes. Add the stock and wine, bring to the boil and cover. Cook over a low heat for about 20 minutes, stirring frequently. Season with salt and nutmeg then sprinkle with parsley.

Serves 4

Poultry Stock

Ingredients	Metric/Imperial
Chicken	1
Lemon grass, chopped	1 stick
Star anis	2 sticks
Cloves garlic, chopped	2
Shallots, finely chopped	4
Dried red chilli peppers, chopped	3
Root ginger, chopped	25 g/1 oz
Carrots, finely chopped	2
Water	3 l/5¼ pts
Fish sauce	15 ml/1 tbsp

1. Wash the chicken, pat dry and cut into small pieces with a sharp knife. Bring the chicken pieces to the boil in a large saucepan with all the remaining ingredients except the fish sauce. Cover and leave to simmer over a low heat for about 3 hours, skimming the froth from the surface. Finally, pour the stock through a sieve and season to taste with fish sauce. Leave the stock to cool and skim off the fat that has set on the top.

Makes 2 l/3½ pts

Soups and Starters

Fennel Soup with Pine Kernels

Ingredients	Metric/Imperial
Fennel bulbs with green tops	450 g/1 lb
Turmeric	10 ml/2 tsp
Coriander	1 sprig
Sesame oil	30 ml/2 tbsp
Pine kernels	100 g/4 oz
Chicken stock	1 l/1¾ pts
Aniseed liqueur	30 ml/2 tbsp
A pinch of sambal oelek	
Oyster sauce	10 ml/2 tsp
Salt	
Freshly ground white pepper	

1. Wash the fennel, cut into strips and toss with the turmeric. Keep the green tops for garnishing. Wash the coriander and remove the leaves from the stalks.
2. Heat 10 ml/2 tsp of oil in the wok. Swirl the oil around then pour it out. Repeat this once more.
3. Heat up the remaining oil in the wok, add the fennel and pine kernels and fry until pale gold. Pour in the chicken stock and cook for 8 to 10 minutes.
4. Add the coriander and season with the liqueur, sambal oelek, oyster sauce, salt and pepper. Serve garnished with the fennel greens.

Serves 4

Preparation time 30 minutes

Photograph opposite (top)

Spinach Soup with Tofu

Ingredients	Metric/Imperial
Fresh spinach leaves	150 g/5 oz
Sesame oil	30 ml/2 tbsp
Clove garlic, thinly sliced	1
Chicken breast, cut into strips	100 g/4 oz
Tofu, cubed	100 g/4 oz
Chicken stock	750 ml/1¼ pts
Salt	
Freshly ground white pepper	
A small pinch of grated nutmeg	
Chives, chopped	1 bunch

1. Clean the spinach and remove the stalks. Wash the leaves and cut them into fine strips.
2. Heat 10 ml/2 tsp of oil in the wok, swirl it around and pour it out. Repeat once more.
3. Heat the remaining oil in the wok, add the garlic, chicken breast and tofu and fry for a minute or so until golden brown. Pour on the chicken stock and simmer for about 10 minutes.
4. Add the spinach to the soup and simmer for about 2 minutes. Season with salt, pepper and nutmeg and serve sprinkled with chives.

Serves 4

Preparation time: 30 minutes

Photograph opposite (bottom)

Sauerkraut Soup with Paprika

Ingredients	Metric/Imperial
Belly pork	225 g/8 oz
Groundnut oil	30 ml/2 tbsp
Shallots, finely chopped	2
Cloves garlic, finely chopped	2
Chilli pepper, chopped	1
Veal or chicken stock	1 l/1¾ pts
Bay leaves	2
Green pepper, diced	1
Sauerkraut, coarsely chopped	225 g/8 oz
Salt	
Freshly ground white pepper	
A pinch of sugar	
Lemon balm	1 sprig

1. Cut the meat into fine strips.
2. Heat 15 ml/1 tbsp of oil in the wok, swirl it around and pour it out again. Repeat once more.
3. Heat the remaining oil in the wok, add the meat, shallots, garlic and the chilli pepper and stir-fry for 5 minutes. Cover with the stock, add the bay leaves, cover and simmer over a low heat for 20 minutes.
4. Add the pepper and sauerkraut and heat through for a further 3 minutes. Season with salt, pepper and sugar then serve garnished with lemon balm.

Serves 4

Preparation time: 30 minutes

Photograph opposite (centre)

Coconut-Chicken Soup with Lychees

Ingredients	Metric/Imperial
Chicken breast	350 g/12 oz
Salt	
Cornflour	10 ml/2 tsp
Groundnut oil	30 ml/2 tbsp
Green chilli pepper, chopped	1
Coconut milk	1 l/1¾ pts
A little grated lemon rind	
Dried lily buds (optional), soaked	10 ml/2 tsp
Lychees, peeled and stoned	12
A pinch of grated nutmeg	
Salt	
Freshly ground black pepper	
Lily blossoms (optional)	4
Lemon balm leaves	2

1. Cut the chicken breast diagonally across the grain into strips. Sprinkle with salt and coat with cornflour.
2. Heat 10 ml/2 tsp of oil in the wok, swirl it round and pour it out again. Repeat once more.
3. Heat the rest of the oil in the wok, add the chicken and chilli pepper and fry for about 15 seconds. Pour on the coconut milk and bring to the boil.
4. Add the lemon rind and the dried lily blossoms, if using. Simmer for 5 minutes.
5. Add the lychees and heat through, then season with nutmeg and salt. Garnish with the fresh lily blossoms, if using, and lemon balm.

Serves 4

Preparation time: 30 minutes

Photograph above left (right)

King Prawn Soup with Sorrel

Ingredients	Metric/Imperial
Peeled king prawns	225 g/8 oz
Salt	
Freshly ground white pepper	
Cornflour	20 ml/4 tsp
Groundnut oil	30 ml/2 tbsp
Carrots, cut into strips	2
Onions, cut into strips	100 g/4 oz
Clove garlic, sliced	1
Chicken stock	750 ml/1¼ pts
Sorrel or spinach, shredded	150 g/5 oz
Shrimp paste	10 ml/2 tsp

1. Wash the prawns, cut them open lengthways to the tail and remove the black intestinal threads. Pat the prawns dry and cut into pieces. Season with salt and pepper then coat with cornflour.
2. Heat 10 ml/2 tsp of oil in the wok, swirl it around then pour it out. Repeat once more. Heat a little more oil in the wok.
3. Increase the heat a little, add the prawns and fry for about 20 seconds. Remove from the wok.
4. Add the carrots, onions and garlic to the wok and fry for 5 minutes. Add the chicken stock and simmer over a low heat for 3 minutes.
5. Add the sorrel or spinach and the prawns and season with shrimp paste, salt and pepper. Serve immediately.

Serves 4

Preparation time: 35 minutes

Photograph above (left)

Goulash Soup with Black Mushrooms

Ingredients	Metric/Imperial
Sirloin steak, trimmed	350 g/12 oz
Salt	
Freshly ground black pepper	
Cornflour	20 ml/4 tsp
Beef tomatoes	2
Dried Mu-err or Chinese mushrooms	50 g/2 oz
Groundnut oil	30 ml/2 tbsp
Onions, cut into strips	200 g/7 oz
Cloves garlic, sliced	2
Red chilli peppers, finely chopped	2
Lemon grass, chopped	1 stick
Bay leaves	2
Dry red wine	250 ml/8 fl oz
Bamboo shoots, drained and chopped	100 g/4 oz
Fresh coriander, chopped	1 sprig
Soy sauce	5 ml/4 tsp
Madeira	15 ml/ 1 tbsp

1. Wash the meat, pat it dry and cut it into fine strips. Season with salt and pepper then coat with cornflour.

2. Cut a cross in the skin at the top of the tomatoes. drop them into boiling water then into cold water. Remove the skins and cut out the base of the stalk. Halve the tomatoes, remove the seeds and cut the flesh into small dice.

3. Soften the Mu-err mushrooms for about 10 minutes in lukewarm water. Drain well and cut off the stalks.

4. Heat 10 ml/2 tsp of oil in the wok, swirl it round and pour out again. Repeat once more.

5. Then heat up the rest of the oil in the wok, add the meat and fry for 2 minutes until golden brown. Add the onions, garlic and chilli peppers and fry all together for 1 minute.

6. Add the mushrooms, lemon grass and bay leaves, pour on the red wine and 750 ml/1¼ pts of water and simmer for about 30 minutes.

7. Stir in the diced tomatoes, bamboo shoots and coriander. Season the soup with soy sauce, Madeira and salt and pepper to taste.

Serves 4

Preparation time: 35 minutes

Chicken Kebab with Soy Bean Sauce

Ingredients Metric/Imperial

For the marinade:

Coriander leaves, finely chopped	12
Lemon leaves, chopped or a little grated lemon rind	2
Red chilli peppers, halved	4
Root ginger, chopped	15 g/½ oz
Lemon grass, chopped	1 stick
Shallots, chopped	50 g/2 oz
Coconut cream	200 ml/7 fl oz
Honey	5 ml/1 tsp
Soy sauce	5 ml/1 tsp
Fish sauce	5 ml/1 tsp
Coriander seeds	5 ml/1 tsp

For the kebab:

Chicken breast	400 g/14 oz
Bacon slices, rinded	4
Sesame oil	60 ml/4 tbsp

For the soy bean sauce

Dried soy beans	50 g/2 oz
Cloves garlic, diced	2
Root ginger, diced	5 ml/1 tsp
Red chilli peppers, halved	2
Soy sauce	10 ml/2 tsp
White wine vinegar	30 ml/2 tbsp
Caster sugar	10 ml/ 2 tsp
Salt	

1. Finely purée the coriander, lemon leaves or rind, chilli peppers, ginger, lemon grass and shallots in a blender with the coconut cream, honey, soy sauce, fish sauce and coriander seeds.
2. Cut the chicken breast diagonally across the grain into 4. Wrap in the bacon rashers then thread on to a skewer. Pour the marinade over the meat and leave to stand for 2 hours.
3. To make the sauce, leave the soy beans to soak for about 1 hour in cold water then drain. Cook the beans in 600 ml/1 pt of water for about 40 minutes until soft. Drain and reserve the water.
4. Purée the beans in a blender with the remaining ingredients and 250 ml/8 fl oz of the water used for cooking the beans. Pour into a small dish.
5. Remove the kebab from the marinade and leave to drain.
6. Heat 10 ml/2 tsp of oil in the wok, swirl it round and pour it out again. Repeat once more.
7. Heat the rest of the oil and fry the kebab for 3 to 5 minutes until cooked and browned, turning occasionally. Serve with the sauce.

Serves 4

Preparation time: 1 hour plus marinating time

Chicken with Ginger and Mushrooms

Ingredients	Metric/Imperial
Chicken breast fillets	250 g/9 oz
Five-spice powder	5 ml/1 tsp
Flour	15 ml/1 tbsp
Groundnut oil	120 ml/4 fl oz
Shallots	50 g/2 oz
Clove garlic, cut into slivers	1
Red Thai ginger or root ginger, cut into strips	50 g/2 oz
Cashew nuts	25 g/1 oz
Honey	5 ml/1 tsp
Rice or potato flour	15 ml/1 tbsp
Rice wine	75 ml/5 tbsp
Mushrooms, quartered	100 g/4 oz
Turmeric	2.5 ml/½ tsp
Yellow chilli peppers, halved	6
Soy sauce	5 ml/1 tsp

Juice of ½ lime
Salt
Freshly ground black pepper
4 leaves iceberg lettuce
A few coriander leaves

1. Cut the chicken breast diagonally across the grain into fine strips, sprinkle with five-spice powder and coat lightly with flour.
2. Heat 10 ml/2 tsp of oil in the wok, swirl it round then pour it out. Repeat once more.
3. Heat a little more oil in the wok, add the strips of chicken and fry for 1 minute or so until golden brown. Remove from the wok and reserve. Pour the oil out of the wok.
4. Add a little more oil to the wok. Add the shallots, garlic, ginger and cashew nuts and fry for about 1 minute. Add the honey and stir round until the vegetables are glazed. Sprinkle the ingredients in the wok with rice or potato flour, add the rice wine and let it briefly soak in, stirring well.
5. Add the mushrooms, turmeric and chilli peppers and cook for about 1 minute. Add the fried chicken and heat through in the sauce. Season with soy sauce, a little lime juice and salt and pepper. Remove from the wok and keep warm.
6. Clean the wok. Heat up a further 10 ml/2 tsp of oil in the wok, swirl it round then pour it out. Repeat once more.
7. Put a little more oil in the wok, add the lettuce leaves and fry quickly. Season with the salt and the remaining lime juice.
8. Arrange the lettuce leaves on a dish and spread the meat and vegetable mixture on top. Garnish with coriander leaves.

Serves 4

Preparation time: 40 minutes

23

Meat Dishes

Whether it is veal, beef, pork or lamb, meat can be beautifully cooked in the wok with a range of all kinds of different ingredients. For the best results, meat is cut into fine strips or thin slices and fried until crispy on the outside while still tender and juicy inside.

Sweet and Sour Pork with Pineapple

Ingredients   Metric/Imperial

For the marinade:

Potato flour	10 ml/2 tsp
Rice wine	10 ml/2 tsp
Soy sauce	10 ml/2 tsp
Sesame oil	10 ml/2 tsp
Salt	
Freshly ground white pepper	
Pork fillet	350 g/12 oz
Small pineapple	1
or	
Canned pineapple, drained	300 g/11 oz
Leek	1
Beef tomatoes, skinned	3
White wine vinegar	10 ml/2 tsp
Honey	10 ml/2 tsp
Small cucumber	1
Groundnut oil	45 ml/3 tbsp
Cloves garlic, chopped	2
Root ginger, chopped	15 g/½ oz
Lemon leaves, or a little grated lemon rind	8
Large red onion, diced	1
Yellow pepper, diced	1
Red chilli peppers, seeded and diced	2
Salt	
Freshly ground white pepper	

1. Stir together the ingredients for the marinade. Cut the fillet of pork into 2.5 cm/1 in cubes and leave to marinate in the sauce in a cool place (not the refrigerator) for about 3 hours, turning at least twice.

2. Cut the top off the pineapple. Peel and cube the fruit.

3. Clean the leek, cut into 2 cm/¾ in pieces and wash well.

4. Halve the tomatoes and remove the seeds. Put the tomato centres on one side. Cut 2 of the tomatoes into large cubes. Purée the third tomato in a blender with the centres, the wine vinegar and honey.

5. Peel the cucumber, quarter it and remove the seeds with a spoon. Cut the cucumber into 2 cm/¾ in pieces.

6. Heat 10 ml/2 tsp of oil in the wok, swirl it round then pour it out. Repeat once more.

7. Heat the remaining oil in the wok. Add the drained meat cubes, the garlic and ginger and fry for 1 to 2 minutes until golden brown. Add the tomato purée and the lemon leaves or rind and simmer for 1 minute.

8. Add the onion, pepper, cucumber and leek and simmer for 3 minutes, stirring.

9. Mix in the pineapple and chilli peppers and simmer for 1 minute. Season well.

Serves 4

Preparation time: 35 minutes plus marinating time

25

Veal with Walnuts and Mushrooms

Ingredients	Metric/Imperial
Veal or turkey breast fillet	400 g/14 oz
Salt	
Freshly ground white pepper	
Juice of orange	1
Flour	15 ml/1 tbsp
Pickled black walnuts with juice	12
Cornflour	5 ml/1 tsp
Groundnut oil	30 ml/2 tbsp
Spring onions, diced	2
Button mushrooms	225 g/7 oz
Medium sherry	45 ml/3 tbsp
Soy sauce	10 ml/2 tsp
Butter	50 g/2 oz
Pine kernels	25 g/1 oz
A few coriander leaves	

1. Cut the fillet of veal or turkey into slices 1 cm/½ in thick. Sprinkle with salt, pepper and orange juice. Dust with flour.
2. Drain and halve the walnuts. Keep the liquid and mix smoothly with the cornflour.
3. Heat 10 ml/2 tsp of oil in the wok, swirl it round then pour it out. Repeat once more.
4. Heat a little oil in the wok, add the veal or turkey strips and fry briskly for about 2 minutes until golden brown. Add the spring onions and mushrooms and fry for about 1 minute.
5. Stir in the sherry and soy sauce then fry for about ½ minute.
6. Stir the walnuts into the cornflour mixture, add to the wok and bring the mixture to the boil. Add the butter in small flakes, but do not allow to boil.
7. Toast the pine kernels in a pan without fat. Season the meat or turkey with salt and pepper and garnish with coriander and pine kernels.

Serves 4

Preparation time: 45 minutes

Photograph opposite (top)

Kidneys with Mustard and Leeks

Ingredients	Metric/Imperial
Veal kidneys	2
Salt	
Freshly ground white pepper	
Flour	15 ml/1 tbsp
Leeks	3
Large potatoes	2
Beef tomatoes, skinned	2
Lean bacon	4 slices
Groundnut oil	150 ml/¼ pt
Root ginger, thinly sliced	25 g/1 oz
Rice or potato flour	10 ml/2 tsp
Veal or chicken stock	150 ml/¼ pt
French mustard	15 ml/1 tbsp
Soy sauce	10 ml/2 tsp
Oyster sauce	10 ml/2 tsp
Basil, chopped	1 bunch

1. Wash the veal kidneys thoroughly under running water. Halve the kidneys along the length, then cut out the nodules of fat and the tubes. Cut the kidneys into thin slices, season with salt and pepper then coat lightly with flour.
2. Clean the leeks, cut into pieces of about 2 cm/¾ in and leave for 10 minutes in cold water. Wash thoroughly and leave to drain well. Wash the potatoes, peel and dice. Cut the tomatoes into quarters and remove the seeds. Snip the rind of the bacon at 1 cm/½ in intervals.
3. Heat 10 ml/2 tsp of oil in the wok, swirl it round then pour it out. Repeat once more.
4. Heat up some more oil in the wok, add the kidney slices and fry gently for about 2 minutes until crispy. Remove from the wok and reserve. Pour out the oil.
5. Add a little more oil to the wok, add the potatoes and fry over a low heat until golden brown. Add the leeks and cook for 2½ minutes over a medium heat. Remove the vegetables and put to one side. Pour out the oil.
6. Add a little more oil to the wok, add the ginger and fry for about ½ minute. Stir in the flour, pour on the stock, add the mustard, the soy and oyster sauce and bring to the boil.
7. Return all the ingredients to the wok with the basil. Fry the bacon in a separate pan until golden brown.
8. Arrange the kidney mixture on a serving dish and garnish with the bacon slices.

Serves 4

Preparation time: 40 minutes

Photograph opposite (bottom)

Beef with Chinese Cabbage

Ingredients	Metric/Imperial
Beef fillet	300 g/11 oz
Salt	
Freshly ground black pepper	
Rice or potato flour	10 ml/2 tsp
Pak soi or Chinese cabbage	300 g/11 oz
Beef tomatoes, skinned	2
Red chilli peppers	2
Groundnut oil	250 ml/ 8 fl oz
Dark brown sugar	5 ml/1 tsp
Red wine vinegar	10 ml/2 tsp
Large onion, cut into strips	1
Cloves garlic, cut into slivers	2
Soy beansprouts	100 g/4 oz
Tomato ketchup	15 ml/1 tbsp
Soy sauce	15 ml/1 tbsp
Fish sauce	45 ml/3 tbsp
Basil leaves	24

1. Cut the beef diagonally across the grain into thin slices. Season with salt and pepper then lightly coat with flour.
2. Remove the outer leaves of the cabbage. Quarter it, cut it into fine strips, wash thoroughly and allow to drain in a sieve.
3. Quarter the tomatoes, remove the seeds and cut the flesh into large cubes. Wash the chilli peppers, halve them, remove the seeds and cut into fine strips.
4. Heat 10 ml/2 tsp of oil in the wok, swirl it round then pour it out. Repeat once more.
5. Heat about half the remaining oil in wok until very hot. Add the beef strips and fry for about 1 minute, stirring all the time. Remove the meat and put to one side. Pour out the oil.
6. Pour the rest of the oil into the wok. Add the sugar with the vinegar and heat until the sugar caramelises.
7. Add the onion, garlic and the chilli peppers and simmer in the liquid for about 2 minutes.
8. Add the cabbage and stir-fry for about 2 minutes. Remove the vegetables and put to one side.
9. Add the beansprouts, ketchup, soy sauce and fish sauce to the wok and stir-fry for about 1 minute.
10. Add the meat, vegetables, tomatoes and 16 basil leaves. Heat through, stirring all the time, for about 1½ minutes.
11. Serve garnished with the remaining basil leaves.

Serves 4

Preparation time: 35 minutes

Pork with Mild Pepperoni

Ingredients	Metric/Imperial
Boned neck of pork	350 g/12 oz
Salt	
Soy sauce	10 ml/ 2 tsp
Thyme	1 sprig
Cornflour	10 ml/2 tsp
Apple	1
Beef tomatoes, skinned	2
Veal or chicken stock	120 ml/4 fl oz
A pinch of sugar	
Leek	1
Groundnut oil	45 ml/3 tbsp
Onions, cut into strips	150 g/5 oz
Mild green peppers, halved	150 g/5 oz
Chives, chopped	½ bunch
Freshly ground black pepper	

1. Cut the neck of pork in cubes about 2 cm/¾ in. Season with salt and sprinkle with soy sauce. Remove the thyme leaves from the stalks and sprinkle over the meat with the cornflour. Set aside for 10 minutes.
2. Peel and halve the apple, remove the core and cut the flesh into small dice.
3. Wash the tomatoes, coarsely chop and put into a blender. Add the stock and sugar then work to a smooth purée. Rub through a mesh sieve for extra smoothness. Clean the leek, cut into little rings, wash well and drain in a sieve.
4. Heat 10 ml/2 tsp of oil in the wok, swirl it round then pour it out. Repeat once more.
5. Heat a little more oil in the wok, add the meat and stir-fry for about 2 minutes until golden brown.
6. Add the onions and peppers and fry briskly for 1 minute. Add the tomato purée and leave to simmer for about 5 minutes until the tomato sauce is thick.
7. Fry the leek and the apple cubes with the other ingredients for about 2 minutes. Season the dish with salt and pepper to taste and serve garnished with chopped chives.

Serves 4

Preparation time: 40 minutes

Pork with Black Beans

Ingredients	Metric/Imperial
Dried black beans	150 g/5 oz
Salt	
Boned neck of pork	350 g/12 oz
Sate spice or five-spice powder	10 ml/2 tsp
Rice or potato flour	20 ml/4 tsp
Red chilli peppers	2
Coriander	1 sprig
Oil	120 ml/4 fl oz
Onions, chopped	225 g/8 oz
Cloves garlic, chopped	2
Large red pepper, chopped	1
Tomato purée	10 ml/2 tsp
Rice wine or dry sherry	30 ml/2 tbsp
Five-spice powder	5 ml/1 tsp
Soy sauce	30 ml/ 2 tbsp
A pinch of grated nutmeg	
Freshly ground black pepper	

1. Leave the beans to soak for about 2 hours in water. Drain and cook in salted water for about 40 minutes until tender but slightly firm to the bite. Drain.

2. Meanwhile, cut the pork into fine strips, sprinkle with the spice and coat lightly with rice or potato flour.

3. Wash the chilli peppers, halve, remove the seeds and cut into fine strips. Remove the coriander leaves from the stalks and chop the leaves finely.

4. Heat 10 ml/2 tsp of oil in the wok, swirl it round then pour it out. Repeat once more.

5. Heat some more oil in the wok. Add the meat and fry quickly for about 2 minutes until golden brown. Remove and leave on one side. Pour out the oil.

6. Heat some more oil in the wok. Add the diced onions and garlic and fry lightly for about 30 seconds. Add the diced pepper and chillis and fry for about 30 seconds. Mix in the tomato purée and the rice wine or sherry.

7. Add the beans and meat to the wok and reheat. Finally, season the dish with the five-spice powder, soy sauce, nutmeg, salt, pepper and sprinkle with the chopped coriander.

Serves 4

Preparation time: 1 hour plus soaking time

Sweet and Sour Lamb

Ingredients	Metric/Imperial
For the marinade:	
Cornflour	10 ml/2 tsp
Plum wine	10 ml/2 tsp
Soy sauce	10 ml/2 tsp
Sesame oil	10 ml/2 tsp
Lemon juice	10 ml/2 tsp
Boned leg of lamb	350 g/12 oz
Cucumber	1
Red chilli peppers	2
Tamarillos or tomatoes	4
Mint	1 bunch
Mango	1
Groundnut oil	45 ml/3 tbsp
Cloves garlic, chopped	2
Root ginger, chopped	15 g/½ oz
Pineapple juice	120 ml/4 fl oz
Wine vinegar	10 ml/2 tsp
Honey	5 ml/1 tsp
Lemon grass, chopped	1 stick
Red onion, diced	
Cornflour	1
White wine	
Salt	10 ml/2 tsp
Freshly ground black pepper	10 ml/2 tsp

1. Mix together all ingredients for the marinade. Cut the lamb into 2 cm/¾ in strips and marinate in a cool place for about 3 hours. Turn several times.
2. Wash the cucumber, halve and remove the seeds with a spoon. Cut the flesh into 2 cm/¾ in pieces. Wash the chilli peppers, halve them, remove the seeds and cut into strips.
3. Wash the tamarillos or tomatoes, peel and quarter. Wash the mint and remove leaves from the stalk. Peel the mango, cut the flesh away from the stone then slice into wide strips.
4. Heat 10 ml/2 tsp of oil in the wok, swirl it round then pour it out. Repeat once more.
5. Heat some more oil in the wok, add the meat, garlic, ginger and chilli peppers and fry for about 2 minutes.
6. Add the pineapple juice, vinegar and honey and leave to cook for about 1 minute. Mix in the lemon grass or rind, the cucumber and the onion. Simmer everything for about 3 minutes.
7. Mix the cornflour smoothly with the wine. Add to the sauce and bring to the boil.
8. Stir in the mango, tamarillos or tomatoes and mint. Season with salt and pepper to taste.

Serves 4

Preparation time: 45 minutes plus marinating time

Lamb with Savoy Cabbage and Mint

Ingredients	Metric/Imperial
Boned leg of lamb	350 g/12 oz
Salt	
Freshly ground black pepper	
Soy sauce	5 ml/1 tsp
Asian mushroom sauce	5 ml/1 tsp
Flour for coating	
Mint	1 sprig
Savoy cabbage	1
Groundnut oil	120 ml/4 fl oz
Large onion, thinly sliced	1
Fruit vinegar	5 ml/1 tsp
Honey	5 ml/1 tsp
A pinch of grated nutmeg	

32

Cold butter	50 g /2 oz
Cloves garlic, thinly sliced	2
Sesame seeds	10 ml/2 tsp
Rice or potato flour	5 ml/1 tsp
Chicken stock	120 ml/ 4 fl oz

1. Cut the lamb into fine strips, sprinkle with salt, pepper, mushroom sauce and soy sauce, then coat with flour.

2. Wash the mint and remove the leaves from the stalks.

3. Halve the cabbage and cut out the stalk. Cut the cabbage into fine strips. Blanch the strips in boiling salted water for about 2 minutes until just tender but still crispy. Plunge into cold water then drain well.

4. Heat 10 ml/2 tsp of oil in the wok, swirl it round then pour it out. Repeat once more.

5. Heat some more oil in the wok until hot. Add the lamb and stir-fry for about 1½ minutes. Remove lamb and leave on one side. Pour out the oil.

6. Heat the rest of the oil in the wok, add the onion slices and fry until golden brown. Add the cabbage strips and fry for a further 1 minute. Stir in the vinegar and honey then season with nutmeg, salt and pepper.

7. Stir in two-thirds of the butter in flakes. Transfer the mixture to a plate and keep it warm.

8. Heat the remaining butter in the wok. Add the garlic and sesame seeds and fry until golden. Mix in the mint. Add the rice or potato flour, stir in well then pour in the stock.

9. Reheat the lamb quickly in the sauce and serve on a separate dish, accompanied by the cabbage.

Serves 4

Preparation time: 40 minutes

Poultry and Game Dishes

Chicken, duck, rabbit, venison — all these meats can be cooked to perfection in the wok with a range of piquant or sweet and sour sauces to delight every palate.

Breast of Duck with Curry Sauce

Ingredients	Metric/Imperial
Duck breasts	2
Salt	
Freshly ground white pepper	
Groundnut oil	120 ml/4 fl oz
Green chilli peppers	2
Lychees	8
Makeur or aubergine	100 g/4 oz
Tamarillos or tomatoes	2
Spring onion	1
Canned bamboo shoots, drained	100 g/4 oz
Honey	5 ml/1 tsp
White wine vinegar	5 ml/1 tsp
Coconut cream	250 ml/8 fl oz
Curry paste	5 ml/1 tsp
Basil leaves	12
Oyster sauce	10 ml/ 2 tsp

1. Make criss-cross cuts in the duck then season with salt and pepper.

2. Heat 10 ml/2 tsp of oil in the wok, swirl it round then pour it out. Repeat once more.

3. Wash the chilli peppers, cut in half, remove the seeds and cut into fine strips.

4. Peel the lychees, halve and remove the stones. Wash the makeur or dice the aubergine. Peel and quarter the tamarillos or tomatoes.

5. Heat 20 ml/4 tsp of oil in the wok. Add the duck and fry for 10 to 15 minutes, turning twice. The meat should remain pink inside. Remove from the wok, cover with aluminium foil and keep warm.

6. Pour the oil out of the wok, swirl around once more with a little more oil then add the remaining oil. Lightly stir-fry the makeur or aubergine, peppers, spring onion, bamboo shoots, honey and wine vinegar for about 2 minutes over a medium heat until transparent.

7. Remove the vegetables from the wok and put on one side. Pour the oil out of the wok and wipe clean with a cloth.

8. Bring the coconut cream to the boil in the wok. Add the curry paste, 8 basil leaves and the oyster sauce, stirring well. Briefly heat up the fried vegetables in the sauce, add the lychees and leave to simmer for about 1 minute.

9. Transfer the vegetables and sauce on to a deep serving plate. Cut the breast of duck into fine slices, arrange on the vegetables then garnish with the tamarillos and remaining basil leaves.

Serves 4

Preparation time: 45 minutes

Chicken with Black Mushrooms and Chinese Cabbage

Ingredients	Metric/Imperial
Chicken legs	4
Lemon juice	15 ml/1 tbsp
Five-spice powder	10 ml/2 tsp
Flour for sprinkling	
Chinese cabbage	1
Groundnut oil	120 ml/4 fl oz
Shallots, sliced	100 g/4 oz
Clove garlic, quartered	1
Poultry stock	250 ml/8 fl oz
Fresh black trumpet mushrooms or ordinary mushrooms	100 g/4 oz
Oyster sauce	10 ml/2 tsp
Mint leaves	12
Rice or potato flour	10 ml/ 2 tsp
White wine vinegar	10 ml/ 2 tsp
Honey	5 ml/1 tsp

Salt
Freshly ground
   black pepper
A pinch of
   sambal oelek

1. Wash the chicken legs, pat dry and sprinkle with a little lemon juice. Rub in the five-spice powder and sprinkle with flour.
2. Cut the Chinese cabbage in half and remove the stalk. Cut the cabbage into strips, wash and leave to drain. Blanch the strips in boiling salted water for about 1 minute, plunge into cold water then leave to drain.
3. Heat 10 ml/2 tsp of oil in the wok, swirl it round then pour it out. Repeat once more.

4. Heat a little more oil in the wok, add chicken legs and fry for about 5 minutes over a medium heat. Add the shallots and garlic and fry for about 30 seconds. Add half the stock and simmer over a low heat for 10 to 15 minutes. Remove the chicken from the wok and keep it warm.
5. Boil the liquid down until well reduced and concentrated. Add the mushroms and cook for about 1 minute. Season with the oyster sauce.
6. Now heat up a little oil in a saucepan and drop in the mint leaves. Stir in the rice or potato flour and the rest of the stock. Season with wine vinegar and honey and cook until thickened.
7. Add the cabbage strips to the sauce and heat through for about 1 minute. Season to taste with salt, pepper and sambal oelek.
8. Arrange the cabbage on a serving plate and place the chicken on top. Serve with the mushrooms and the sauce.

Serves 4

Preparation time: 45 minutes

Chicken with Almonds, Lychees and Mango

Ingredients	Metric/Imperial
Chicken breasts	400 g/14 oz
Five-spice powder	5 ml/ 1 tsp
Rice or potato flour	10 ml/ 2 tsp
Lychees	100 g/4 oz
Red chilli peppers	2
Mango	1
Groundnut oil	250 ml/8 fl oz
Almonds	50 g/2 oz
Carrot, sliced	1
Cloves garlic, chopped	2
Shallots, cut into strips	2
Brown sugar	10 ml/2 tsp
Honey	2.5 ml/½ tsp
Red wine vinegar	10 ml/2 tsp
Poultry stock	120 ml/ 4 fl oz
Fish sauce	10 ml/2 tsp
Coriander leaves	12

1. Cut the chicken breast into thin strips diagonally across the grain. Mix the five-spice powder with half the rice or potato flour and use to coat the chicken strips.

2. Peel the lychees, halve and remove the stones. Halve the chilli peppers, remove the seeds and cut into fine strips.

3. Wash and peel the mango. Remove the flesh from the stone and cut into wide strips.

4. Heat 10 ml/2 tsp of oil in the wok, swirl it round then pour it out. Repeat once more.

5. Heat half the remaining oil in the wok, add the strips of chicken breast and fry for about 2 minutes until crispy. Remove from the wok and put to one side. Pour out the oil.

6. Pour the remaining oil into the wok. Add the almonds, carrot, garlic, chilli peppers and shallots. Fry for about 1 minute.

7. Add the sugar and honey and fry over a high heat until the sugar has caramelised. Pour in the wine vinegar, stock and fish sauce and bring to the boil. Stir the remaining flour with a little cold water until smooth. Add to the pan, mix in well and bring back to the boil.

8. Add the lychees, chicken and coriander. Reheat briefly and arrange on a deep plate. Toss the mango pieces for about 10 seconds in the wok without adding extra oil and use as a garnish.

Serves 4

Preparation time: 45 minutes

Chicken in Garlic

Ingredients	Metric/Imperial
Small fresh chickens	2
Cloves garlic, finely chopped	8
Rosemary	1 sprig
Dry white wine	450 ml/¾ pt
Olive oil	45 ml/3 tbsp
Salt	
Freshly ground white pepper	
Iceberg lettuce	1
Flat-leaf parsley or parsley	1 bunch
Groundnut oil	120 ml/4 fl oz
Cold butter	75 g/3 oz

1. Wash the chickens inside and out, wipe dry and then cut them in half.

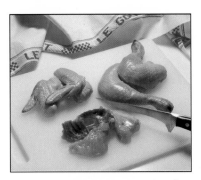

2. Separate the legs and the wings from the carcass and, using a knife, chop all remaining parts, with the bones, into 5 cm/ 2 in pieces.

3. Mix together the garlic, rosemary, wine, olive oil, salt and pepper in a bowl, add the chicken, cover and marinate for about 6 hours in the refrigerator.

4. Separate the leaves of the iceberg lettuce, wash and drain well. Wash the parsley and chop finely.

5. Drain the chicken pieces well, reserving the marinade. Rub the marinade through a sieve.

6. Heat 10 ml/2 tsp of oil in the wok, swirl it round then pour it out. Repeat once more.

7. Heat some more of the oil in the wok. Add all the chicken and fry for about 5 minutes until brown. Remove from the wok and keep warm. Pour out the oil.

8. Cook the marinade in the wok for about 1 minute then add the parsley. Stir in small flakes of butter with a whisk. Reheat without boiling. Keep the sauce warm.

9. Heat remaining oil in the wok, add the lettuce and fry lightly. Season with salt and pepper. Arrange the lettuce on a plate, distribute the chicken pieces on top and coat with sauce.

Serves 4

Preparation time: 25 minutes plus marinating time

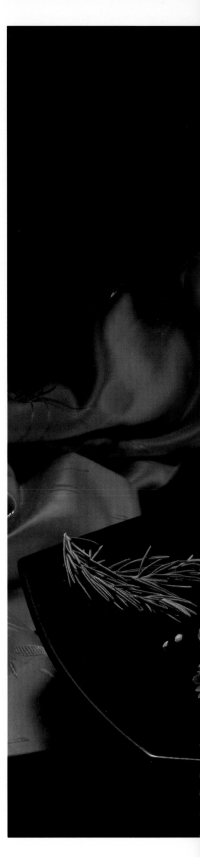

38

Spring Rolls with Coconut and Chicken

Ingredients	Metric/Imperial
Rice leaves or filo pastry sheets	24
Coconut chips	100 g/4 oz
Chicken breast fillets	200 g/7 oz
Salt	
Freshly ground white pepper	
Cornflour	10 ml/2 tsp
Groundnut oil	500 ml/18 fl oz
Spring onion, sliced	1
Root ginger, chopped	15 g/½ oz
Clove garlic, chopped	1
Soy beansprouts	50 g/2 oz
Coconut cream	30 ml/2 tbsp
Curry paste	2.5 ml/½ tsp
Soy sauce	5 ml/1 tsp

1. Soften the rice leaves, if using, one at a time for about 30 seconds in cold water. Then lay them out next to each other on a piece of kitchen paper and drain.
2. Soak the coconut chips in boiling water for about 10 minutes then drain. Cut the skinned chicken into strips. Sprinkle with salt and pepper then coat with cornflour.
3. Heat 10 ml/2 tsp of oil in the wok, swirl it round then pour it out. Repeat once more.
4. Heat a little more oil in the wok and stir-fry the chicken for about 20 seconds. Add the spring onion, ginger, garlic, coconut chips and beansprouts and fry for about 30 seconds. Season with salt, pepper, coconut cream, curry paste and soy sauce, pour into a bowl and leave to cool.
5. Put equal amounts of the vegetable and meat filling in the centre of each rice leaf or filo pastry sheet. Fold the lower edge of the leaves over the filling, then the two edges towards the centre. Roll the rice leaves or pastry together. Press the edges together well.
6. Heat the remaining oil in the cleaned wok and fry the spring rolls for 1½ to 2 minutes, take them out and drain on kitchen paper. Red Chilli Sauce (page 16) goes well with this dish.

Serves 4

Preparation time: 45 minutes

Photograph opposite (top)

Rice Pockets with Prawns and Pineapple

Ingredients	Metric/Imperial
Rice leaves or filo pastry sheets	24
Bean noodles	100 g/4 oz
Shelled prawns	175 g/6 oz
Salt	
Freshly ground white pepper	
Cornflour	10 ml/2 tsp
Pineapple	100 g/4 oz
Groundnut oil	500 ml/18 fl oz
Spring onion, sliced	1
Root ginger, chopped	15 g/½ oz
Coriander, chopped	1 sprig
Shrimp paste	5 ml/1 tsp
Soy sauce	5 ml/1 tsp

1. Soften the rice leaves, if using, one at a time for 30 seconds in cold water, then lay them out on kitchen paper and leave to drain.
2. Soak the bean noodles in hot water for 10 minutes then drain.
3. Cut the prawns into fine cubes, sprinkle with salt and pepper and dust with cornflour. Peel and dice fresh pineapple, or drain and dice canned pineapple.
4. Heat 10 ml/2 tsp of oil in the wok, swirl it round then pour it out. Repeat once more.
5. Heat some more oil in the wok and stir-fry the prawns for 10 seconds. Add the pineapple, spring onion, ginger and coriander and stir-fry for 1 minute.
6. Add the bean noodles, season with shrimp paste, soy sauce, salt and pepper and leave to cool.
7. Place equal quantities of filling on each of the rice leaves or pastry sheets. Fold up the bottom edges over the filling, turn the two side edges inwards and roll the rice leaves or pastry together. Press the edges firmly.
8. Heat the remaining oil in the cleaned wok and fry the rice pockets for about 1½ minutes. Remove them from the wok and drain on kitchen paper. Chilli-Spice Sauce (page 16) goes well with this dish.

Serves 4

Preparation time: 40 minutes

Photograph opposite (bottom)

Duck with White Mushrooms and Bamboo Shoots

Ingredients	Metric/Imperial
Dried morel mushrooms	8
Duck breast fillets	400 g/14 oz
Salt	
Freshly ground white pepper	
Chilli peppers	2
Coriander	1 sprig
Groundnut oil	45 ml/3 tbsp
Coconut cream	200 ml/7 fl oz
Curry paste	5 ml/1 tsp
Shallots, sliced	2
Chives, chopped	1 bunch
Fish sauce	10 ml/2 tsp
Cornflour	10 ml/2 tsp
Rice wine	10 ml/2 tsp
Canned bamboo shoots, chopped	175 g/6 oz

1. Soak the mushrooms for about 10 minutes in hot water.
2. Make criss-cross cuts in the duck and season with salt and pepper.
3. Wash the chilli peppers, halve them, remove the seeds and cut the peppers into pieces. Wash the coriander and remove the

leaves from the stalk.
4. Heat 10 ml/2 tsp of oil in the wok, swirl it round then pour it out. Repeat once more.
5. Heat some more oil in the wok, add the duck and fry on both sides for about 8 minutes. Remove from the wok and put to one side.
6. Heat the coconut cream in the wok. Add the drained morel mushrooms, the curry paste and shallots and simmer for about 5 minutes. Stir in the chilli peppers, coriander, chives and fish sauce. Season with salt and pepper.
7. Stir the cornflour smoothly with rice wine or sherry. Add to the sauce in the wok and cook until the sauce is thickened. Stir in the bamboo shoots.
8. Cut the duck fillets into slices, add to the sauce and reheat for about 1 minute.

Serves 4

Preparation time: 50 minutes

Photograph opposite (bottom)

42

Duck with Braised Pineapple

Ingredients	Metric/Imperial
Duck breast fillets	400 g/14 oz
Soy sauce	10 ml/2 tsp
Sambal oelek	10 ml/2 tsp
Rice wine	120 ml/4 fl oz
Salt	
Freshly ground white pepper	
Rice or potato flour	20 ml/4 tsp
Small pineapple or	1
Canned unsweetened pineapple	300 g/11 oz
Groundnut oil	45 ml/3 tbsp
Root ginger, finely chopped	15 g/½ oz
Honey	10 ml/2 tsp
White wine vinegar	5 ml/1 tsp
Carrots, sliced	100 g/4 oz
Green pepper, diced	1
Tomato ketchup	20 ml/4 tsp

1. Cut the duck fillets into 2 cm/½ in pieces. Mix the soy sauce with the sambal oelek, 10 ml/2 tsp of rice wine, salt and pepper in a bowl to make the marinade. Sprinkle the duck with rice or potato flour, add to the marinade and mix well. Marinate for 30 minutes.
2. Meanwhile, cut the top off the pineapple, peel the fruit carefully, halve and cut out the stalk. Cut the flesh into small cubes. Alternatively, drain and dice the canned pineapple.
3. Heat 10 ml/2 tsp of oil in the wok, swirl it round then pour it out. Repeat once more.
4. Heat some more oil in the wok, add the duck cubes and fry briskly for about 1 minute until crispy. Remove from the wok and keep warm.
5. Roast the ginger in the wok for about 10 seconds, then add the honey, wine vinegar and remaining rice wine.
6. Add the pineapple cubes, carrot slices, diced pepper and ketchup. Simmer for 2 minutes. Finally add the duck pieces and reheat before serving.

Serves 4

Preparation time: 35 minutes plus marinating time

Photograph opposite (top)

家 禽 水 牛

羊 羔 汤

Venison with Broccoli and Pine Kernels

Ingredients	Metric/Imperial
Boned venison	350 g/12 oz
Salt	
Freshly ground black pepper	
Flour	15 ml/1 tbsp
Broccoli florets	200 g/7 oz
Lean bacon	75 g/3 oz
Groundnut oil	120 ml/4 fl oz
Pine kernels	50 g/2 oz
Mango chutney	75 g/3 oz
Dry red wine	45 ml/3 tbsp
Chicken stock	120 ml/4 fl oz
Cinnamon	1 stick
A pinch of grated nutmeg	
A small pinch of sambal oelek	
Dried figs, halved	100 g/4 oz

1. Cut the venison into 1 cm/ ½ in thick slices. Season with salt and pepper, then coat with flour.

2. Blanch the broccoli in boiling water for 3 minutes then plunge into cold water and drain.

3. Cut the bacon into wide strips.

4. Heat 10 ml/2 tsp of oil in the wok, swirl it round then pour it out. Repeat once more.

5. Heat some more oil in the wok, add the venison and stir-fry briskly for 2 minutes until brown. Remove the venison and pour out the oil.

6. Heat the remaining oil in the wok. Add the bacon rashers and pine kernels and fry for about 20 seconds until brown. Mix in the mango chutney, stirring over a low heat all the time.

7. Pour in the red wine, stock, cinnamon stick and sambal oelek. Simmer until the liquid is reduced by half.

8. Add the venison, broccoli and figs to the sauce and reheat. Season with nutmeg, salt and pepper.

Serves 4

Preparation time: 40 minutes

Photograph opposite (top)

Rabbit with Crayfish and Mango

Ingredients	Metric/Imperial
Rabbit joints	4
Cloves garlic, halved	2
Salt	
Freshly ground white pepper	
Cornflour for dusting	
Crayfish tails	8
Mango	1
Fresh lychees	12
Mint	1 bunch
Groundnut oil	120 ml/4 fl oz
Red chilli peppers, halved	2
Root ginger, sliced	15 g/½ oz
Large carrot, sliced	1
Rice or potato flour	10 ml/2 tsp
Mild mustard	10 ml/2 tsp
Sugar	2.5 ml/½ tsp
Plum wine	120 ml/4 fl oz
Juice of lime	1

1. Bone the rabbit joints and remove the sinews. Cut the flesh into 3 cm/1¼ in pieces. Rub the garlic into the meat then season with salt and pepper and dust with cornflour.

2. Cut the upper sides of the crayfish tails along the length and remove the black intestinal threads. Wash the crayfish, pat dry and season to taste with salt and pepper. Dust with a little flour.

3. Peel the mango, cut the flesh away from the stone then slice into wide strips. Peel the lychees, remove the stones and halve the flesh. Wash the mint and remove the leaves from the stalk.

4. Heat 10 ml/2 tsp of oil in the wok, swirl it round then pour it out. Repeat once more.

5. Heat some more oil in the wok, add the rabbit and fry on all sides over a medium heat for about 4 minutes until brown. Remove from the wok and keep warm. Pour out the oil.

6. Heat some more oil in the wok, add the crayfish and mint leaves and fry for about 30 seconds. Remove and leave on one side.

7. Lightly fry the chilli peppers and ginger in the wok then add the carrot slices. Sprinkle the vegetables with rice or potato flour and mix in well. Add the mustard, sugar and plum wine to the wok and stir into the vegetables.

8. Add the mango, lychees and rabbit to the wok and heat through for about 1 to 2 minutes. Transfer to a serving dish.

9. Add the crayfish to the wok, season with lime juice, salt and pepper. Then heat for a few seconds, turning. Arrange on the rabbit and vegetables.

Serves 4

Preparation time: 40 minutes

Photograph opposite (bottom)

44

Fish Dishes

For lovers of fine fish dishes, cooking with a wok is ideal, as fish can be cooked perfectly in a wok, losing none of its delicate flavour. The selection of dishes in this chapter will offer something to suit everyone's taste.

Salmon in Red Curry Sauce with Green Paprika

Ingredients	Metric/Imperial
Salmon fillet	400 g /14 oz
Salt	
Freshly ground white pepper	
Soy sauce	10 ml/2 tsp
Cornflour	20 ml/4 tsp
Groundnut oil	45 ml/3 tbsp
Green peppers, diced	2
Red onion, diced	1
Clove garlic, diced	1
Coconut cream	200 ml/7 fl oz
Curry paste	10 ml/2 tsp
Paprika	5 ml/1 tsp
Red pepper-corns	5 ml/1 tsp
Coriander, chopped	1 sprig
Fish sauce	5 ml/1 tsp

1. Wash the salmon, pat it dry and cut it into 3 cm/1½ in pices. Sprinkle with salt, pepper and soy sauce. Coat lightly with cornflour.

2. Heat 10 ml/2 tsp of oil in the wok, swirl it round then pour it out. Repeat once more.

3. Heat some more oil in the wok, add the salmon cubes and fry lightly for about 1 minute until pale gold. Remove from the wok and put to one side.

4. Add the peppers, onion and garlic to the wok and fry for 1½ minutes. Add the coconut cream, curry paste, paprika, peppercorns and coriander and leave to simmer gently for about 2 minutes. Season with fish sauce.

5. Return the salmon to the sauce and reheat very gently for about 1 minute. Transfer the salmon and vegetables to a serving plate.

6. Whisk the sauce lightly and then spoon it over the fish.

Serves 4

Preparation time: 35 minutes

Sole with Baby Sweetcorn

Ingredients	Metric/Imperial
Sole fillets	300 g/11 oz
Salt	
Freshly ground white pepper	
Juice of lemon	1
Cornflour	20 ml/4 tsp
Groundnut oil	45 ml/3 tbsp
Leek, chopped	1
A small piece root ginger, sliced	
Baby sweetcorn	200 g/7 oz
Mangetout	100 g/4 oz
Dried lily blossoms (optional)	5 ml/1 tsp
Sugar	5 ml/1 tsp
Lemon grass, shredded	1 stick
Chicken stock	30 ml/2 tbsp
Tomato ketchup	10 ml/2 tsp
Soy sauce	10 ml/2 tsp
Fish sauce	10 ml/2 tsp
Green peppercorns	5 ml/1 tsp
Coriander leaves	8
Fresh lily blossoms (optional)	8

1. Wash the sole, pat dry and cut into 3 cm/1½ in pieces. Sprinkle with salt, pepper and half the lemon juice, then dust with cornflour.
2. Heat 10 ml/2 tsp of oil in the wok, swirl it round then pour it out. Repeat once more.
3. Heat some more oil in the wok, add the sole and fry for 1 to 2 minutes until golden brown on both sides. Remove from the wok and put to one side.
4. Fry the leek and ginger briefly in the wok. Add the sweetcorn, mangetout and dried lily buds, if using, then sweeten lightly with a little sugar. Add the lemon grass, the remaining lemon juice and the chicken stock. Bring to the boil and simmer for 1 minute.
5. Season the vegetables with the tomato ketchup, soy sauce, fish sauce and peppercorns. Return the fish to the wok.
6. Reheat the fish gently over a low heat for 1 minute then transfer to a serving plate and garnish with coriander and fresh lily blossoms, if using.

Serves 4

Preparation time: 35 minutes

Photograph opposite (top)

Sole on Chinese Cabbage with Almonds

Ingredients	Metric/Imperial
Sole fillet	400 g/14 oz
Salt	
Freshly ground white pepper	
Juice of lemon	1
Cornflour	30 ml/2 tbsp
Eggs	2
Flaked almonds	50 g/2 oz
Chinese cabbage, shredded	1
Flat-leaf parsley	1 bunch
Groundnut oil	120 ml/4 fl oz
Cloves garlic, thinly sliced	2
Lemon leaves or a little lemon rind	4
Coconut cream	90 ml/6 fl oz
Rice-schnaps or vodka	10 ml/2 tsp
Fish sauce	10 ml/2 tsp

1. Wash the sole, pat it dry and cut it into 4 cm/2 in pieces. Sprinkle with salt, pepper and lemon juice then coat with cornflour.
2. Whisk the eggs with 10 ml/2 tsp of the remaining cornflour and a little salt. Use to coat the fish, then toss them in the flaked almond until each piece is well covered.
3. Blanch the Chinese cabbage in boiling salted water for about 1 minute then plunge it into cold water. Leave to drain well. Wash the parsley and remove leaves from stalks.
4. Heat 10 ml/2 tsp of oil in the wok, swirl it round then pour it out. Repeat once more.
5. Heat some more oil in the wok, add the garlic slices and lemon leaves or grated rind and fry for about ½ minute. Add the cabbage and fry for 2 minutes. Pour in the coconut cream and cook for about 1½ minutes.
6. Blend the remaining cornflour smoothly with schnaps or vodka, add to the wok and bring to the boil. Season the vegetables with salt, pepper and fish sauce. Transfer to a serving dish and keep warm.
7. Clean the wok, swirl 10 ml/2 tsp of oil round it then pour out.
8. Heat some more oil in the wok, add the sole and fry for about 2 minutes until crispy. Remove and reserve.
9. Fry the parsley briefly in the hot oil. Arrange the pieces of sole on the cabbage and garnish with the fried parsley.

Serves 4

Preparation time: 40 minutes

Photograph opposite (bottom)

48

Ginger Haddock with Pak Soi

Ingredients	Metric/Imperial
Haddock fillet	400 g/14 oz
Salt	
Freshly ground white pepper	
Pak soi or Chinese cabbage	200 g/7 oz
Groundnut oil	45 ml/3 tbsp
Root ginger, thinly sliced	15 g/½ oz
Red onion, chopped	1
Dried red chilli peppers	2
Honey	5 ml/1 tsp
Tomato ketchup	10 ml/2 tsp
Malt vinegar	10 ml/2 tsp
Dry white wine	30 ml/2 tbsp
Soy sauce	10 ml/2 tsp
Fish sauce	10 ml/2 tsp
Oyster sauce	10 ml/2 tsp
Shrimp paste	5 ml/1 tsp
A few chervil leaves	

1. Skin the haddock then cut into 2 cm/¾ in pieces. Sprinkle with salt and pepper.

2. Clean the cabbage and cut it into small pieces.

3. Heat 10 ml/2 tsp of oil in the wok, swirl it round then pour it out. Repeat once more.

4. Heat some more oil in the wok, add the ginger and fry for 30 seconds. Add the onion, cabbage and chilli peppers. Fry for another 1 minute. Stir in the honey, ketchup, vinegar and wine.

5. Add the haddock pieces to the vegetables and cook for 2 minutes. Season with soy, fish and oyster sauces and shrimp paste. Garnish with chervil.

Serves 4

Preparation time: 35 minutes

Plaice with Bacon and Gherkins

Ingredients	Metric/Imperial
Plaice fillets	400 g/14 oz
Salt	
Freshly ground white pepper	
Cornflour	30 ml/2 tbsp
Groundnut oil	45 ml/3 tbsp
Honey	5 ml/1 tsp
Onion, chopped	1
Borage leaves, chopped	8
Pickled cucumbers, drained and chopped	200 g/7 oz
Lean bacon, chopped	100 g/4 oz
Pickled pearl onions	100 g/4 oz
Shrimp paste	5 ml/1 tsp
Chicken stock	30 ml/2 tbsp
Peeled prawns	75 g/3 oz
Dill, chopped	1 sprig
Borage blossoms (optional)	20

1. Wash the plaice fillets, pat dry and cut into 3 cm/1¼ in pieces. Sprinkle with salt and pepper, then coat in half the cornflour.
2. Heat 10 ml/2 tsp of oil in the wok, swirl it round then pour it out. Repeat once more.
3. Heat some more oil in the wok, add the fillets and fry briskly for 30 seconds. Remove from the wok and reserve.
4. Put the honey into the wok with the onion, borage, pickled cucumbers, bacon and pearl onions. Mix the shrimp paste and remaining cornflour into the stock, add to the wok and bring to the boil, stirring.
5. Return the fish to the wok, add the prawns and briefly reheat. Garnish with dill and borage blossoms, if using.

Serves 4

Preparation time: 30 minutes

King Prawns with Kaiso Algae

Ingredients	Metric/Imperial
Dried Kaiso algae	20 g/¾ oz
Fresh king prawns	12
Salt	
Freshly ground white pepper	
Cornflour	20 ml/4 tsp
Groundnut oil	45 ml/3 tbsp
Root ginger, finely chopped	15 g/½ oz
Spring onions, sliced	2
Tomato juice	30 ml/2 tbsp
Lemon grass, chopped	1 stick
Tamarillos or tomatoes, quartered	2
Coriander leaves	20
Soy sauce	5 ml/1 tsp
Fish sauce	5 ml/1 tsp
Raspberry vinegar	5 ml/1 tsp

1. Cut the algae in 2 cm/¾ in pieces using scissors. Place in cold water for about 10 minutes then drain.

2. Wash the prawns, remove the tails from the shells, cut along the length up to the tail and remove the black intestinal threads. Sprinkle with salt and pepper then coat with cornflour.

3. Heat 10 ml/2 tsp of oil in the wok, swirl it round then pour it out. Repeat once more.

4. Heat some more oil in the wok, add the prawns and fry for about 1 minute. Remove from the wok and keep warm.

5. Fry the ginger quickly in the wok for about 10 seconds. Add the spring onions and fry for about 20 seconds. Mix in the tomato juice and lemon grass and simmer for 1½ minutes.

6. Stir in the algae, tamarillos or tomatoes and coriander. Season with soy and fish sauces and raspberry vinegar. Return the prawns to the wok and reheat briefly with the vegetables.

Serves 4

Preparation time: 40 minutes

King Prawns with Mango Chutney

Ingredients	Metric/Imperial
Fresh king prawns	12
Salt	
Freshly ground white pepper	
Juice of lemon	1
Cornflour	30 ml/2 tbsp
Mango	1
Mustard powder	5 ml/1 tsp
Honey	5 ml/1 tsp
Coconut cream	30 ml/2 tbsp
Sambal manis	5 ml/1 tsp
Mild Indian curry powder	30 ml/2 tbsp
Chicken stock	120 ml/4 fl oz
Groundnut oil	120 ml/4 fl oz
Cloves garlic, finely chopped	2
Spring onions, chopped	2
Bulb fennel, chopped	1
Mango chutney	100 g/4 oz
Nasturtium blossoms (optional)	6

1. Wash the prawns, remove the tails from the shells, cut them open along their length to the tails and remove the black intestinal threads. Sprinkle with salt, pepper and lemon juice then coat with half the cornflour.

2. Peel the mango, cut the flesh away from the stone then dice the flesh.

3. Mix the mustard powder with the honey, coconut cream, sambal manis, curry powder, the rest of the cornflour and the chicken stock.

4. Heat 10 ml/2 tsp of oil in the wok, swirl it round then pour it out. Repeat once more.

5. Heat some more oil in the wok. Add the garlic, spring onions and fennel and fry for 2 minutes. Stir in stock, bring to the boil and simmer for 1 minute.

6. Mix in the mango cubes and chutney. Season with salt. Arrange the vegetables in a deep serving plate and keep warm. Clean the wok.

7. Heat some more oil in the wok. Add the prawns and fry for 2 minutes. Arrange the prawns on the vegetables then garnish with greenery from the fennel and nasturtium blossoms, if using.

Serves 4

Preparation time: 35 minutes

King Prawns with Courgettes and Lychees

Ingredients	Metric/Imperial
Fresh king prawns	12
Salt	
Freshly ground white pepper	
Soy sauce	10 ml/2 tsp
Cornflour	10 ml/2 tsp
Lychees	12
Groundnut oil	45 ml/3 tbsp
Cloves garlic, thinly sliced	4
Red chilli peppers	2
Courgettes, diced	200 g/7 oz
Spring onion, chopped	1
Coconut cream	120 ml/4 fl oz
A few coriander leaves	
Mild curry powder	10 ml/2 tsp
Fish sauce	5 ml/1 tsp

1. Wash the prawns, remove the tails from the shells, cut them open along the length up to the tails and take out the black intestinal threads. Sprinkle with salt, pepper and soy sauce, then coat with cornflour.

2. Peel the lychees, halve and remove stones.

3. Heat 10 ml/2 tsp of oil in the wok, swirl it round then pour it out. Repeat once more.

4. Heat some more oil in the wok, add the prawns and fry for about 1 minute. Add the garlic and chilli peppers, followed by the courgettes, spring onions and lychees. Fry for about 1 minute. Remove the contents of the wok and reserve. Clean the wok.

5. Put the coconut cream into the wok and cook for about 1½ minutes until thick. Stir in the coriander, curry powder, fish sauce and salt and pepper to taste.

6. Warm up the prawns and vegetables in the sauce. Remove the whole chillis before serving.

Serves 4

Preparation time: 40 minutes

King Prawns with Black Walnuts

Ingredients	Metric/Imperial
Fresh king prawns	12
Salt	
Freshly ground black pepper	
Juice of lemon	1
Cornflour	30 ml/2 tbsp
Pickled walnuts with juice	12
Groundnut oil	30 ml/2 tbsp
Walnut oil	30 ml/2 tbsp
Leek, sliced	1
Canned bamboo shoots, drained and chopped	100 g/4 oz
Lemon leaves or a little grated lemon rind	4
Chicken stock	150 ml/¼ pt
Chives, chopped	1 bunch
Soy sauce	10 ml/2 tsp
A few mint leaves	

1. Wash the prawns, remove the tails from the shells, cut them open along the length up to the tails and take out the black intestinal threads. Sprinkle with salt, pepper and lemon juice, then coat with half the cornflour.
2. Drain the walnuts and keep the juice. Halve the nuts and dust with the remaining cornflour.
3. Heat 10 ml/2 tsp of groundnut oil in the wok, swirl it round then pour it out. Repeat once more.
4. Heat the remaining groundnut oil and some walnut oil in the wok, add the prawns and fry for about 30 seconds. Remove from the wok and reserve.
5. Fry the leek in the wok quickly with the walnuts, bamboo shoots and lemon leaves or lemon rind, allowing about 45 seconds. Add the chicken stock, bring to the boil and simmer for 1 minute.
6. Add the walnut juice and bring the mixture to the boil Return the prawns to the wok and reheat for about 1 minute. Stir in the chives and season with soy sauce. Garnish the dish with mint leaves.

Serves 4

Preparation time: 45 minutes

Vegetarian Dishes

Vegetable dishes as main courses or to accompany other dishes can be cooked beautifully in the wok, making the most of the wonderful range of vegetables available in the shops and markets.

56

Fried Vegetables with Honey

Ingredients	Metric/Imperial
Groundnut oil	45 ml/ 3 tbsp
Small piece of root ginger, chopped	
Cloves garlic, sliced	2
Fresh or canned baby sweetcorn, drained	100 g/4 oz
Spring onions, sliced	2
Red pepper, diced	1
Green pepper, diced	1
Mushrooms, halved	100 g/4 oz
Honey	10 ml/2 tsp
Fruit vinegar	10 ml/2 tsp
A pinch of sambal oelek	
Soy sauce	10 ml/2 tsp
Salt	
Freshly ground white pepper	
A few coriander leaves	
A few lily blossoms (optional)	

1. Heat 10 ml/2 tsp of oil in the wok, swirl it round then pour it out. Repeat once more.

2. Heat some more oil in the wok, add the ginger and garlic and fry for 30 seconds. Add the rest of the vegetables with the mushrooms and stir-fry for about 30 seconds.

3. Mix in the honey, vinegar, sambal oelek and soy sauce. Season with salt and pepper. Add the coriander, arrange the vegetables on a serving dish and garnish with lily blossoms, if using.

Serves 4

Preparation time: 35 minutes

Onions with Parmesan

Ingredients	Metric/Imperial
Groundnut oil	20 ml/4 tsp
Unsalted butter	30 ml/2 tbsp
White bread, cubed	150 g/5 oz
Red onions, sliced	450 g/1 lb
Crème frâiche	
Chicken stock	120 ml/4 fl oz
Parmesan cheese, grated	150 ml/¼ pt 100 g/4 oz
Salt	
Freshly ground white pepper	
Grated nutmeg	
Bay leaves	
Chervil leaves, chopped	4 4

1. Heat 10 ml/2 tsp of oil in the wok, swirl it round then pour it out. Repeat once more.

2. Heat a little butter in the wok, add the bread cubes and fry until golden brown. Remove from the wok and reserve. Wipe out the wok with kitchen paper to remove any leftover breadcrumbs.

3. Heat some more butter in the wok, add the onions and fry for about 30 seconds. Mix the crème frâiche with the stock and Parmesan and season with salt, pepper and nutmeg. Add this to the wok with bay leaves and bring to the boil. Cover the wok with a lid and simmer for 4 minutes.

4. Season with salt and pepper and remove the bay leaves. Finally, garnish with the bread cubes and chervil.

Serves 4

Preparation time: 20 minutes

Photograph (top)

Pearl Onions in Orange-Ginger Sauce

Ingredients	Metric/Imperial
Oranges	3
Red chilli peppers	2
Walnut oil	45 ml/3 tbsp
Pearl onions	600 g/1¼ lb
Root ginger, chopped	15 g/½ oz
Sugar	10 ml/2 tsp
Cider vinegar	10 ml/2 tsp
Red pepper-corns	15 ml/1 tbsp
Salt	
Lemon leaves or a little grated lemon rind	4
A few coriander leaves	

1. Wash the oranges in hot water and, using a grater, cut the peel into narrow slivers. Halve the oranges and squeeze out the juice. Wash the chilli peppers, halve and remove the seeds.
2. Heat 10 ml/2 tsp of oil in the wok, swirl it round then pour it out. Repeat once more.
3. Heat some more oil in the wok, add the onions, ginger and chilli peppers. Stir-fry for about 30 seconds. Stir in the sugar then simmer the vegetables in the wok until transparent.
4. Mix in the orange juice, cider vinegar, peppercorns and orange rind. Season with salt.
5. Stir in the lemon leaves or lemon rind. Reserve a few coriander leaves then add the rest. Arrange in a serving dish then garnish with the reserved coriander leaves.

Serves 4

Preparation time: 30 minutes

Photograph (centre)

59

Shallots in Malt Beer

Ingredients	Metric/Imperial
Walnut oil	45 ml/3 tbsp
Small shallots	600 g/1¼ lb
Brown sugar	10 ml/2 tsp
Red pepper-corns	5 ml/1 tsp
Malt beer	250 ml/8 fl oz
Balsamic vinegar	45 ml/3 tsp
Salt	
Freshly ground black pepper	
Paprika	
A lamb's lettuce	

1. Heat 10 ml/2 tsp of oil in the wok, swirl it round then pour it out. Repeat once more.
2. Heat some more oil and fry the shallots until golden brown. Add the sugar and cook, stirring, until transparent.
3. Add the peppercorns, beer and vinegar and simmer for 1 minute. Season then garnish with lettuce.

Serves 4

Preparation time: 20 minutes

Photograph (bottom)

Peppers with Tofu

Ingredients	Metric/Imperial
Large red pepper	1
Large green pepper	1
Onions	150 g/5 oz
Basil	1 bunch
Parsley	1 bunch
Beef tomatoes, skinned	2
Salt	
Freshly ground white pepper	
Sambal oelek	1 pinch
Soy sauce	10 ml/2 tsp
Olive oil	45 ml/3 tbsp
Tofu, cubed	200 g/7 oz

1. Wash and halve the peppers, remove the seeds and cut flesh into strips. Peel the onions and cut into rings. Wash the basil and parsley and keep a few leaves for garnishing. Chop the rest finely.

2. Quarter the tomatoes, remove the seeds and purée flesh in a blender with the salt, pepper, sambal oelek and soy sauce.
3. Heat 10 ml/2 tsp of oil in the wok, swirl it round then pour it out. Repeat once more.
4. Heat some more oil in the wok. Add the tofu cubes and fry for 1½ minutes until golden brown. Add the pepper strips and onion rings and fry for 2 minutes.
5. Add the tomato purée, mix in well and cook the ingredients for 1 minute. Season with salt and pepper, then stir in the chopped herbs. Garnish with the reserved basil and parsley.

Serves 4

Preparation time: 30 minutes

Photograph (bottom left)

Braised Carrots with Honey

Ingredients	Metric/Imperial
Small spring carrots	1 kg/2 lb
Coriander	1 bunch
Groundnut oil	20 ml/4 tsp
Unsalted butter	20 ml/4 tsp
Honey	10 ml/2 tsp
Pine kernels	100 g/4 oz
Salt	
Freshly ground white pepper	

1. Wash the carrots and cut the green down to 5 mm/¼ in. Remove the coriander leaves.
2. Heat 10 ml/2 tsp of oil in the wok, swirl it round then pour it out. Repeat once more.
3. Heat the butter add the honey with 15 ml/1 tbsp of water and bring to the boil. Add the carrots and cook for 3 to 4 minutes.

4. Add the coriander and pine kernels then season.

Serves 4

Preparation time: 20 minutes

Photograph (top right)

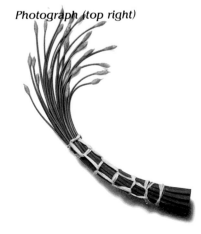

Mushrooms in Curry Sauce

Ingredients	Metric/Imperial
Dried Mu-err mushrooms	50 g/2 oz
White morel mushrooms	50 g/2 oz
Oyster mushrooms	200 g/7 oz
Button mushrooms	400 g/14 oz
Groundnut oil	45 ml/3 tbsp
Cloves garlic, chopped	2
Shallots, finely chopped	2
Coconut cream	200 ml/7 fl oz
Curry paste	10 ml/2 tsp
A little soy sauce	
Salt	
Freshly ground white pepper	
Flat-leaf parsley, chopped	1 bunch

1. Soak the Mu-err and the morel mushrooms in lukewarm water for 10 minutes. Drain. Quarter the oyster and button mushrooms.
2. Heat 10 ml/2 tsp of oil in the wok, swirl it round then pour it out. Repeat once more.
3. Heat some more oil in the wok, add the garlic and shallots and fry for 1 minute. Add the mushrooms and continue to cook for another minute.
4. Stir in the coconut cream and curry paste then simmer for 3 minutes.
5. Season with soy sauce, salt and pepper then sprinkle with chopped parsley.

Serves 4

Preparation time: 30 minutes

Photograph opposite (top)

Mushrooms with Black Walnuts

Ingredients	Metric/Imperial
Shiitake mushrooms	600 g/1¼ lb
Pickled black walnuts with juice	16
Cornflour	10 ml/2 tsp
Green basil leaves	16
Red basil leaves	8
Walnut oil	45 ml/3 tbsp
Spring onions, sliced	2
Soy sauce	10 ml/2 tsp
Fish sauce	10 ml/2 tsp
Salt	
Freshly ground black pepper	

1. Clean and wash the mushrooms and leave to drain. Drain the walnuts and reserve the juice. Halve the nuts. Mix the juice smoothly with the cornflour.
2. Cut the green basil into fine strips. Wash the red basil.
3. Heat 10 ml/2 tsp of oil in the wok, swirl it round then pour it out. Repeat once more.
4. Heat some more oil in the wok, add the mushrooms and spring onions then fry for 2½ minutes. Add the walnuts with their juice and cook for about 30 seconds.
5. Add the green basil with the soy and fish sauces then season with the salt and pepper. Garnish with the red basil leaves.

Serves 4

Preparation time: 20 minutes

Photograph opposite (centre)

Mushrooms with Anchovy Sauce

Ingredients	Metric/Imperial
Small mushrooms	600 g/1¼ lb
Shallots	2
Beef tomato, skinned	1
Olive oil	45 ml/3 tbsp
Lemon grass, chopped	1 stick
Flat-leaved parsley, chopped	1 bunch
Anchovy paste	20 ml/4 tsp
Cold butter	60 g/2½ oz
Salt	
Freshly ground black pepper	
White bread	4 slices
Anchovy fillets, drained	8

1. Clean the mushrooms. Peel the shallots and cut into thin rings. Halve the tomato, remove the seeds and dice the flesh.
2. Heat 10 ml/2 tsp of oil in the wok, swirl it round then pour it out. Repeat once more.
3. Heat some more oil in the wok, add the mushrooms, shallots and lemon grass and fry for 30 seconds until brown.
4. Add the diced tomato and half the parsley and stir well. Mix in the anchovy paste and butter in small piees. Season with salt and pepper.
5. Toast the bread until golden brown then sprinkle with the remaining parsley. Arrange the anchovy fillets on top and serve with the mushrooms.

Serves 4

Preparation time: 25 minutes

Index to Recipes

64

foulsham

Yeovil Road, Slough,
Berkshire, SL1 4JH

ISBN 0-572-01767-7

This English language edition
copyright © 1992 W. Foulsham &
Co. Ltd

Originally published by Falken-
Verlag, GmbH, Niedernhausen TS,
Germany.

Photographs copyright ©
Falken-Verlag

Phototypeset in Great Britain by Typesetting Solutions,
Slough, Berks.
Printed in Portugal.